3/02

PROJECT MERCURY

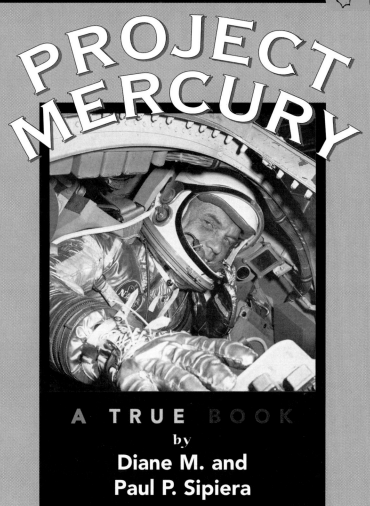

A TRUE BOOK

by

**Diane M. and
Paul P. Sipiera**

Children's Press®
A Division of Grolier Publishing

New York London Hong Kong Sydney
Danbury, Connecticut

A Project Mercury
space capsule

Subject Consultant
Peter Goodwin
*Science Department Chairman
Kent School, Kent, CT*

Reading Consultant
Linda Cornwell
*Learning Resource Consultant
Indiana Department of
Education*

*Authors' Dedication:
To William L. Vidmar
for his years of dedicated
service to his students*

Library of Congress Cataloging-in-Publication Data

Sipiera, Diane M.
    Project Mercury / by Diane M. Sipiera and Paul P. Sipiera.
    p. cm. — (A true book)
    Includes bibliographical references and index.
    Summary: Describes early space exploration and the six missions of
Project Mercury that constituted America's first step toward the moon.
    ISBN 0-516-20443-2 (lib.bdg.)   0-516-26275-0 (pbk.)
    1. Project Mercury (U.S.)—Juvenile literature. [1. Project Mercury
(U.S.) 2. Astronauts.] I. Sipiera, Paul P. II. Title. III. Series.
TL789.8.U6M483 1997
629.45'4'0973—dc21
                                                        96-37919
                                                          CIP
                                                          AC

Contents

Icarus's father watches Icarus fly too close to the Sun in the Greek myth.

Looking to Space

People have dreamed of space flight for more than two thousand years. In an ancient Greek myth, a boy named Icarus made wings out of feathers and wax so that he could fly. His flight was a success until he flew too close to the Sun. The Sun's heat melted the wax, and his wings fell apart.

During the late 1400s to the 1600s, people such as Leonardo da Vinci and Galileo Galilei dreamed of flying, too. They wondered what it would be like to travel to the Moon.

In 1865, a Frenchman named Jules Verne wrote about a trip to the Moon. In his book, a spaceship was launched from Florida and traveled around the Moon.

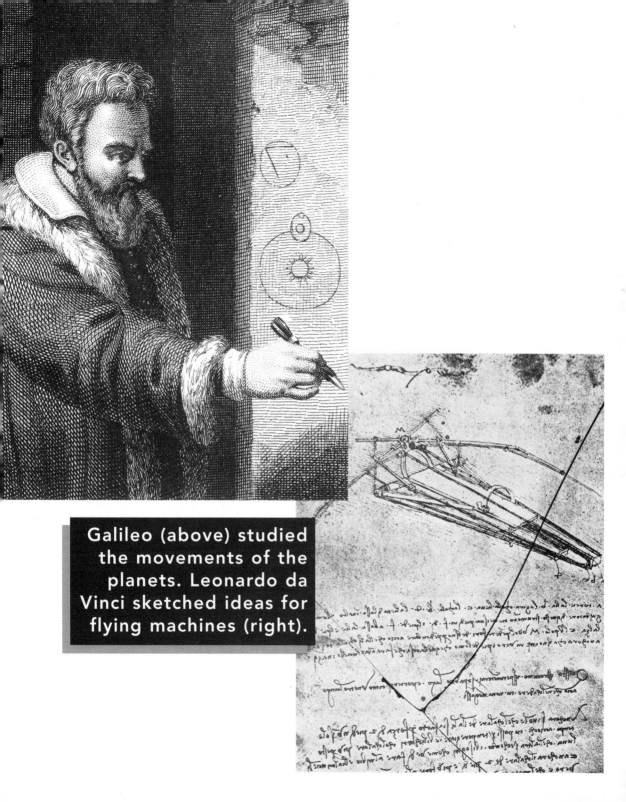

Galileo (above) studied the movements of the planets. Leonardo da Vinci sketched ideas for flying machines (right).

In his book *From the Earth to the Moon*, Jules Verne imagined passengers on a trip into space.

Three men and two dogs rode inside. Although the story was fiction, Verne had predicted the future.

A Space Program

Before a rocket carried a person into space, people were flying to the edge of space. The United States designed a plane called the *X-15* that could fly faster and higher than ever before. Many of its pilots flew higher than 50 miles (80 kilometers) above the earth.

Pilots, such as Chuck Yeager (right), proved that planes could fly faster and higher than ever before. The *X-15* (above) flew to the edge of space.

At that height, they could see the blackness of space above them and the curve of the earth below. Some of these pilots later became astronauts.

The U. S. space program began in 1958. It was based on a study of German rockets from World War II (1939–45). The United States planned a slow and careful development of rockets that someday

Researchers developed spacecraft to place satellites, such as this one, into orbit around the earth.

would put satellites into orbit. Later, the rockets could put people into orbit, too.

The Soviet Union also had a space program. The Soviets were the first to travel beyond our planet. On October 4, 1957, they sent a satellite, called *Sputnik I*, into orbit around the earth.

After the launch of *Sputnik I*, the United States tried to launch a satellite of its own. But the first rocket exploded

Sputnik I (left) was the first satellite in space. The United States's first try at launching a satellite ended when the spacecraft blew up on the launch pad (below).

on the launch pad. The first successful U.S. flight took place on January 31, 1958, when the *Explorer I* satellite went into orbit. A "space race" between the United States and the Soviet Union had begun.

The first person in space was a Soviet cosmonaut, Yuri Gagarin. He was launched on April 12, 1961, and made one orbit around the earth. Gagarin's achievement

Yuri Gagarin was the first person to orbit the earth.

caused the world to believe that Soviet science was better than that of the United States.

Preparing to Explore

The Soviet success caused the
United States to speed up its
plans for space exploration.
The first step was to organize a
new space program. In April
1958, President Dwight D.
Eisenhower helped form the
National Aeronautics and
Space Administration (NASA).

NASA's headquarters in Houston, Texas (above), and Washington, D.C. (right)

NASA's job was to send the United States into space.

NASA began by taking over several projects run by the army and navy. And after several successful satellite launches in 1958, Project Mercury was born. This special program was designed to place a manned space capsule into orbit around the earth, preparing NASA for travel to the Moon and beyond.

Placing an astronaut into earth orbit would not be easy. Many problems had to be solved before a launch could take place. Rockets powerful enough to orbit a manned capsule had to be built. Researchers had to plan and test how the

Powerful rockets carried Mercury capsules into space. The capsule is the black cone at the top of the rocket.

capsule would land, and how it would be recovered after it splashed down in the ocean. Tracking stations had to be set up around the world to keep in constant contact with the

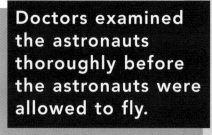

astronauts. Most importantly, methods to keep a person alive in space had to be developed. Astronauts had to go through intense medical tests to see if they could fly in space. No one knew how the human body would react to space conditions.

Splashdown!

NASA planned a way for the astronauts and capsules to be recovered after their flights. After orbiting the earth, Mercury capsules would reenter the earth's atmosphere and land in the ocean. Three parachutes would be on board each capsule—two to help it land and one for emergencies. The astronauts would be picked up by helicopters.

The Mercury Astronauts

After testing hundreds of volunteers, NASA selected seven people to be the Mercury astronauts. They were: Alan B. Shepard Jr., Virgil I. Grissom, John H. Glenn Jr., M. Scott Carpenter, Walter M. Schirra Jr., L. Gordon Cooper Jr., and Donald K. Slayton. Each of these men had been a

The Mercury astronauts could not be more than 5 feet 11 inches (1.8 meters) in height. The capsule could not fit someone taller.

pilot in the military and had a college degree in science or engineering. As astronauts, they also would have to become experts in spacecraft design.

Project Mercury

Alan B. Shepard Jr.

Virgil I. Grissom

John H. Glenn Jr.

M. Scott Carpenter

Walter M.
Schirra Jr.

L. Gordon Cooper Jr.

Donald K.
Slayton

Mission	Astronauts	Launch Date
Mercury-Redstone 3	Shepard	May 5, 1961
Mercury-Redstone 4	Grissom	July 21, 1961
Mercury-Atlas 6	Glenn	February 20, 1962
Mercury-Atlas 7	Carpenter	May 24, 1962
Mercury-Atlas 8	Schirra	October 3, 1962
Mercury-Atlas 9	Cooper	May 15, 1963

Space was an unexplored environment, so astronauts had to be trained to deal with new experiences, such as weight-lessness and the increased gravity at launch and reentry. They planned for every possi-ble situation. At the end of their training, the astronauts were ready for almost anything.

Before a person could be launched, however, both the rocket that would shoot him into space and the capsule that

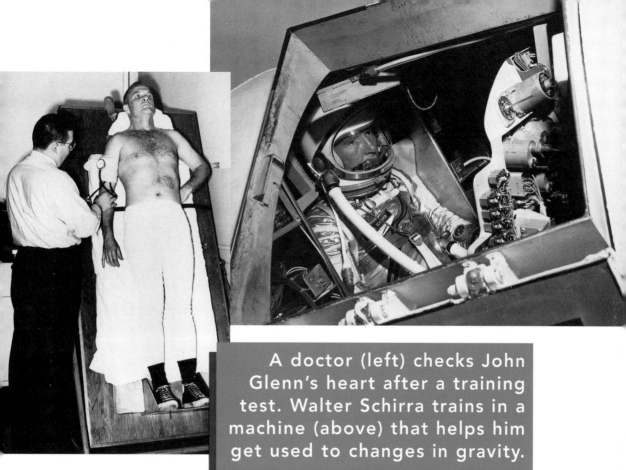

A doctor (left) checks John Glenn's heart after a training test. Walter Schirra trains in a machine (above) that helps him get used to changes in gravity.

would carry him had to be tested. On December 19, 1960, a Mercury capsule on top of a Redstone rocket was launched successfully.

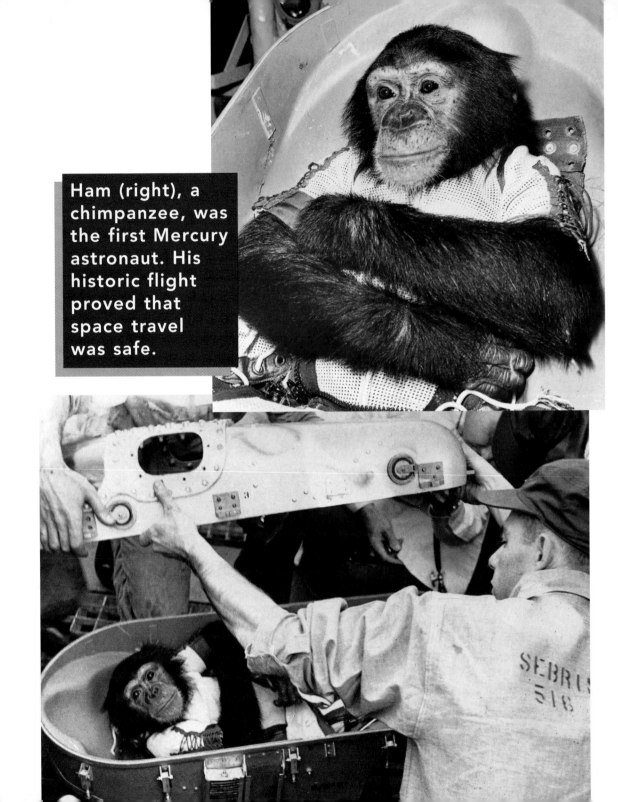

Ham (right), a chimpanzee, was the first Mercury astronaut. His historic flight proved that space travel was safe.

The next Mercury flight had a passenger. He was a three-year-old chimpanzee named Ham. Ham's flight lasted only eighteen minutes, and he experienced six and a half minutes of weightlessness. During his short flight, Ham performed all of his tasks well. His flight helped NASA know how a person would function in space.

Shepard, Grissom, and Glenn

Less than one month after Gagarin became the first person in space, the United States launched Alan B. Shepard Jr. on May 5, 1961. His flight did not place him into orbit like Gagarin. It took him 116 miles (187 km) high, and he was weightless for about five minutes.

A Mercury-Redstone rocket launched Alan Shepard into space (left). After Shepard's flight, President John F. Kennedy (below right) awarded him NASA's Distinguished Service Medal.

The second American in space was Virgil (Gus) I. Grissom. His flight was a repeat of Shepard's mission. The launch and flight went well, and Grissom splashed down in the

A technician checks Gus Grissom's space capsule before launch (left). Splashdown (below) did not go smoothly for Grissom. He was saved, but the capsule sank.

Atlantic Ocean as expected. But then, something went wrong. As Grissom was preparing to leave the capsule, the hatch blew open without warning. Water rushed in, and Grissom quickly escaped. A helicopter tried to raise the capsule. Grissom was saved, but the spacecraft sank into the ocean.

The first Mercury astronaut in orbit was John H. Glenn Jr. He was launched into space on February 20, 1962. His mission was a success, lasting almost five hours as he completed three orbits.

John Glenn trains for his flight (left). At age thirty-seven, he was the oldest of the seven Mercury astronauts.

Glenn did have several problems during the flight. When his automatic controls failed, he had to fly the spacecraft himself. He had another problem when he fired his reentry rockets. His instruments showed that the heat shield might have fallen off the capsule. Without the shield, the spacecraft would burn up. Luckily, the instruments were wrong, and Glenn returned to a hero's welcome.

Because Glenn was the first American to orbit the earth, he was given a parade in New York City.

Flying Through Space

The Mercury capsule was only 6 feet (1.8 meters) across at its widest end, so it was a tight squeeze for an astronaut. At first, the capsule did not have a window. But for the second Mercury flight, a window was added for the astronaut to look out into space.

NASA was not sure if astronauts in flight

would be able to swallow food, or if they would choke. So the astronauts were given food that was like baby food in a tube. John Glenn was the first Mercury astronaut to eat in space.

Carpenter, Schirra, and Cooper

M. Scott Carpenter was the next American in orbit, launched on May 24, 1962. Carpenter's flight completed three orbits. He experienced many minor problems during the mission. The worst problem occurred during reentry when

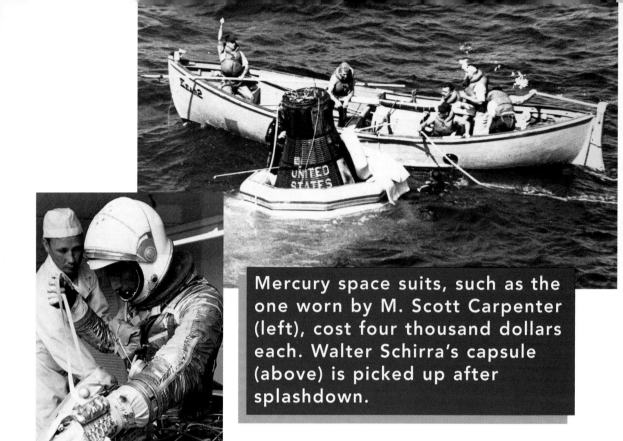

Mercury space suits, such as the one worn by M. Scott Carpenter (left), cost four thousand dollars each. Walter Schirra's capsule (above) is picked up after splashdown.

Carpenter did not fire his rockets on time. He missed his landing site by 250 miles (402 km), and it took almost two hours for the recovery ship to find him.

Astronaut Walter M. Schirra Jr. was next, launching into space on October 3, 1962. There was a problem with the rocket during launch, but once in orbit, things went better. He did have some trouble with his space suit when he couldn't control its temperature. Because Schirra was an expert in space-suit design, he quickly solved the problem. Schirra orbited five and three-quarter times and splashed down in the Pacific Ocean.

The sixth and last Mercury astronaut to be launched into space was L. Gordon Cooper Jr. on May 15, 1963. His mission achieved NASA's goal of keeping a person in orbit for one full day. During his flight, Cooper was able to see many details on the earth's surface, and most of the experiments he performed were successful.

Cooper's mission lasted long enough for him to take a seven-hour nap, but the mood changed after the nineteenth orbit. Cooper's automatic

L. Gordon Cooper was the last Mercury astronaut in space. He took the first pictures of the earth from this new view.

control system failed, and he had to land the spacecraft entirely on his own. Cooper performed perfectly and proved how important it was to have a pilot at the controls.

Project Mercury

After Cooper's successful mission,
Project Mercury officially ended
on June 12, 1963. Donald K.
Slayton, the seventh Mercury
astronaut, did not fly a mission.
He became an astronaut on
future NASA flights.

Project Mercury succeeded in
placing six people into space.
The six missions totaled 2 days,

When Project Mercury ended after the last flight (left) the United States was closer to reaching the Moon (right).

5 hours, 55 minutes, and 27 seconds of manned space flight. The total cost of the project was $392 million. Project Mercury proved that human beings could survive in space and prepared NASA for future missions. It was the United States's first step toward the Moon.

To Find Out More

Here are more places to learn about space exploration:

 **Books**

 **Organizations**

Abernathy, Susan. **Space Machines.** Western Publishing, 1991.

Kerrod, Robin. **The Story of Space Exploration.** Dutton Children's Books, 1994.

Morris, Ting and Neil. **Space.** Franklin Watts, 1994.

Richardson, James. **Science Dictionary of Space.** Troll Associates, 1992.

Sipiera, Diane M. and Paul P. **Project Gemini.** Children's Press, 1997.

The Planetary Society
65 North Catalina Avenue
Pasadena, CA 91106
(818) 793-5100
http://planetary.org

NASA Teacher Resource Center
Mail Stop 8-1
NASA Lewis Research Center
21000 Brookpark Road
Cleveland, OH 44135
(216) 433-4000

National Space Society
922 Pennsylvania Avenue SE
Washington, DC 20003
(202) 543-1900

**National Air and
Space Museum**
Smithsonian Institution
601 Independence Avenue SW
Washington, DC 20560
(202) 357-1300

Online Sites

**The Children's Museum
of Indianapolis**
*http://childrensmuseum.
org/sq1.htm*

Visit the SpaceQuest
Planetarium to see what it
has to offer, including a
view of this month's night
sky. It can connect you to
other astronomy Web sites,
too.

**History of Space
Exploration**
*http://bang.lanl.gov/
solarsys/history.htm*

This site has a helpful time-
line of space exploration
and tells the history of the
spacecraft and astronauts.

Kid's Space
*http://liftoff.msfc.nasa.gov/
kids/welcome.html*

Space exploration is really
fun at this Web site. Find
out how much you would
weigh on the Moon, play
games, solve puzzles, take
quizzes, read stories, and
look at the gallery of pictures drawn by kids. Find
out how you can post a
drawing online, too!

NASA Home Page
http://www.nasa.gov

Visit NASA to access infor-
mation about its exciting
history and present
resources.

The Nine Planets
*http://seds.lpl.arizona.edu/
nineplanets/nineplanets/
nineplanets.html*

Take a multimedia tour of
the solar system and all of
its planets and moons.

Important Words

capsule a small spacecraft holding one or more astronauts

gravity the force of attraction between two objects

manned when there are people on board a spacecraft

mission a goal for spacecraft or astronauts to accomplish

orbit the path a spacecraft travels around the earth

reentry when a spacecraft passes through the earth's atmosphere to land

rocket a powerful vehicle that launches capsules into space

satellite an object that orbits the earth

weightlessness the appearance of astronauts and objects floating in space

Index

Meet the Authors

Paul and Diane Sipiera are a husband and wife who share interests in nature and science. Paul is a professor of geology and astronomy at William Rainey Harper College in Palatine, Illinois. He is a member of the Explorers Club, the New Zealand Antarctic Society, and was a member of the United States Antarctic Research Program. Diane is the director of education for the Planetary Studies Foundation of Algonquin, Illinois. She also manages and operates the STARLAB planetarium program for her local school district.

When they are not studying or teaching science, Diane and Paul can be found enjoying their farm in Galena, Illinois, with their daughters, Andrea, Paula Frances, and Carrie Ann.